TRIBUTE TO THE ADVENT

A Collection of Christmas Poems

William R. Mitchell

Illustrations By

William James Brown

Tribute to the Advent
by William R. Mitchell

Illustrations by William James Brown

Some poems were previously published as *Voices Of The Advent.*

Cross Timbers Books (http://crosstimbersbooks.com)

ISBN: 978-0-557-08306-0

Printed in the United States of America

Fifth Edition

Contents

Preface

In December of 1973 I was sitting at my desk addressing Christmas cards to fellow teachers at Oklahoma Baptist University. I had bought a box of cards illustrated with the familiar "peaceable kingdom" motif. As I looked at that illustration over and over, a line of poetry came to me, which I hurriedly wrote down:

> In that kingdom where a little child
> shall lead us, force and love shall be at home,
> reconciled.

I went on to finish the poem that is reprinted here on page 19, and copied it onto each of the cards I had addressed. Every year since then, I have written a poem to send to friends and family at Christmas; they are collected here for the first time. These poems have been a blessing and a discipline for me. I hope that for others also they may help strip away confusion and custom that have dulled the Advent season and obscured from us the beauty and significance of the birth of Jesus.

As the years have gone by, I have discovered something about the various participants in the original Advent drama. The coming of Jesus seems to have presented each of them with the demand to respond in some sacrificial or sacramental way. If they did so, they were themselves transfigured into something new and holy. Thus even in the cradle Jesus called those whom he encountered to redefine themselves in his own image, as he continues to do for all who genuinely encounter him. And so may it be for us all.

I would like to thank two of my colleagues at OBU—Jim Brown for his sensitive illustrations and Steve Hicks for the calligraphy. My gratitude also to the many friends and family who have encouraged me through the years. Finally, I am grateful for a grant from the Joe and Adeanya Hunt Fund which helped make this publication possible.

1989

Preface to the Second Edition

The generous reception of the first edition has encouraged us to bring out an expanded version. This new edition adds nine poems and illustrations, products of the years 1989 through 1997, to the original sixteen. We are again indebted to Steve Hicks for the calligraphy.

It has been a quarter of a century now since this series began. We have changed; our lives have been checkered with joy and sorrow, triumph and failure. But the beauty of Christ's incarnation has grown steadily more intense, richer yet more simple, as these verbal and visual interpretations try to show. May the joy and peace of the birth of Jesus come to you also through our offering – that is our purpose and our prayer.

1998

*To all those metaphors of Jesus
who have blessed and cheered my life*

Tribute to the Advent

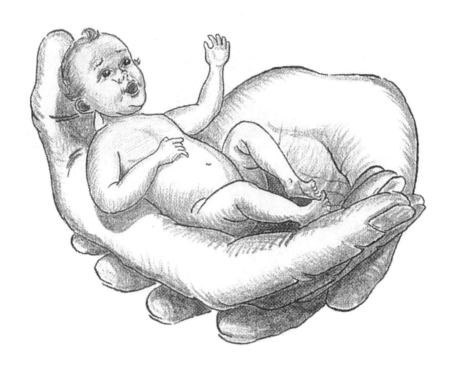

and the glory of the Lord shall be
Revealed,
and all flesh shall see it together

Isaiah 40:5

Immanuel

And God said, How can they understand,
        their eyes blinded by blood, their ears
        stunned with blasphemies?
Not even the psalmist's loveliest rhapsodies,
        the fragrance of the forest, the statement of sunrise,
        can speak my love through their loud guilt and fears.

I will write my law of love in the dust of the earth
I will make it alive and yielding with my tears
I will knead it and form it gently in my hand
I will utter it in a poem of human birth
        and He shall be bone of my spirit,
          He shall be breath of my voice,
       and all flesh shall see it and hear it
          together, and know, and rejoice.

and on earth
PEACE

good will toward men

Luke 2:14

God's Noel

Go down, angels, to the anguished earth—
quiet the shepherds, startled by your wings,
so quick to fear, hardened by sufferings—
       tell of this birth.

       Speak joy to them—
tell of the sign that waits in Bethlehem
in a crude manger, swaddled in mere clay—
      there every wildered mortal may
       hear a carol sung
of heaven's making, rhymed in human tongue.

Comfort my people, coax them from their fear—
      go sweetly sing,
     "Sharing, assuaging humanhood
     exults, exalts, the heavenly King!"
Sing, "Peace is come to men who love the good—
      Be of good cheer!"

let us now go even unto Bethlehem,
and see this thing which is come to pass,
which the LORD hath made known
unto us   Luke 2:15

Shepherds' Song

Dear little mother, we have come
      only to behold—
we will not touch his lovely face,
      our hands are rude and cold;

and we were only watching sheep
      huddled against the snow,
where David waited for the dawn
      ten thousand griefs ago

and one was searching in the wilds
      a sheep that strayed apart,
stumbling through wearisome ravines,
      anxious and sick of heart

and one was making shelter
            for a labor–burdened ewe,
a warmth where she might lay her young
            (as all good shepherds do)

and I was listening to the flocks,
            like wildered children, plead
in almost human voices
            their almost human need

and I was speaking comfort
            in the lonely, bitter night
(as shepherds must) when suddenly
            the skies were burst with light

and the old, old hills of Judea
      and the cold of a thousand years
were laden with joy and singing,
      and so we forgot our fears
and we kneeled down on the barren ground
      and shouted and laughed in our tears

and so we have come to Bethlehem
      to wish our savior well—
but why the cheeriest winter–song
      that ever men befell
should come to shepherds in their fields,
      Lady, we cannot tell.

The dayspring from on high
hath visited us,
To give light to them that sit in darkness
and in the shadow of death,
To guide our feet into the way of

PEACE   Luke 1: 78-79

The Way of Peace

All that men learned from sacred scrolls
was broken faith and twisted souls—
the heritage of noble halls
was broken swords and blackened walls—
So Love invaded guile and war,
      misery and unease;
into our darkness came a star,
      into our anger, peace.

But men forget that heavenly grace
makes every stall a princely place,
and trust to reap from iron force
joy, mercy, or remorse;
and so, good Christians, let us pray
      in thought and work and hymn:
"Lord, make each morn a Christmas day,
      each heart a Bethlehem."

We have seen his STAR
in the east, and are come to
WORSHIP him
Matthew 2:2

Wise Man

What if a man should study till old age,
    till he became a sage—

What if one dazzling mystery
    should seize his mind
    and bid him rise and go afar
    and risk his wisdom and his destiny
    against all common sense
    on the mere witness of a star—

What if he gathered up his everything
    and bartered it for frankincense
    (because one does not come before a king
    in empty–handed insolence)—

What if he carried it in aching hands
    through frozen, empty lands,
    his limbs grown weak, his eyes gone nearly blind,
    until his way should lead
    only where cattle feed—

What then if he should find
his God knows how to give a gift, as well as humankind?

because there was no room
for them in the inn

Luke 2:7

Stable Boy

Counting shekels in the candle–light,
      reconciling his account, my master labored late,
and I sat drowsing in the chilly night,
      keeping the gate.

Dull cold lay on my shoulders like warm hay—such
      as I pull around me where I make my bed—
so that I dreamed I slept. I woke to the touch
      of hands laid gently on my bowing head.

A dusty Nazarene, and a tired girl on a colt,
      asking for shelter at the crowded inn.
I knew the answer, but I drew the bolt
      and went within—

I thought, maybe he'll rent them his own bed,
        if only for his greed,
and sleep himself in the upper room instead
        kept ready for the rich man's need—

but no—just glanced up quickly from his gold,
        waved them away and smiled.
I watched them stumble out into the cold.
        I saw she was with child.

I had a vision of a wayside birth
        in a raw ditch, and not a hand to care—
I took them to the only bed on earth
        was mine to share.

And mine it is, and none can say we stole—
       not that I own the stable, by man's law,
but even the fox finds shelter in a hole,
       even the lambs have straw,

and mother and child shall have a stall for borning,
       and I will pay due rental on demand—
merely to sit awake in the cold till morning,
       warmed with a peace I cannot understand.

and a little CHILD shall lead them...
They shall not hurt nor destroy
in all my holy mountain

Isaiah 11:6-9

The Peaceable Kingdom

In that kingdom where a little child
  shall lead us, force and love shall be at home,
   reconciled.
By still waters they shall lie together.
Justice and mercy then shall kiss each other.
Strength will be more than wrath and lust for blood,
kindness more than stratagem or weakness,
  humility not merely pride exiled,
   and more than shame our meekness.
O Lion of Judah, O thou Lamb of God, thy Kingdom come.

PREPARE ye the WAY
of the LORD

Isaiah 40:3
Mark 1:3

Mary among the Cattle

Make ready, said the voice,
      prepare your heart, your womb,
make him a cradle, make a temple,
      make the Lord room—
and all my ready body said, Amen,
      let it be so.

Make ready, said the voice to Abraham,
      arise and go—
make ready, said the prophet long ago,
      make all the desert bloom—
make him an altar, make him a kingdom,
      make him a psalm.

Find him a shelter in a cattle shed,
      lend him a stall——
throw a little straw together, make a bed.
This is the Author of Orion, Shepherd of the Pleiades—
      let all the cattle kneel.

Pity the poor unready world, my love—
      they know not what they do.
Wise men bring their spice and gold,
the cattle give their huddled warmth,
      their quiet moan, their breath—
in a world of loneliness and cold,
      broken trust and death,
which is the greater gift, I think I know.
Take my cloak around you, love, my coat also,
and if, to soothe the corners of this rough–hewn world
      it can give comfort, fold
      and break my body too.

Yea,
a sword shall pierce
through thy own soul
also

Luke 2:35

Mother and Child

Before she drowsed from weariness
she heard the wind moan through the shed
her tuneless lullaby went dead
her hand fell limp in its caress
light from the candle on the wall
folded softly round his head
the shadows of the cattle–stall
patterned a cross upon his bed

Not to the stable on - ly Christ came down

But to all things lone - ly in Beth - le'm town -

Blind and lame and weary, All whose lives were dreary

Not to the stable on - ly Christ came down.

WORDS AND MUSIC BY WILLIAM MITCHELL

Come unto me, ALL YE that labour
and are heavy laden,
and I will give you rest

Matthew 11:28

Christ Came Down

Not to the stable only
     Christ came down,
but to all things lonely
     in Bethlehem town—
blind and lame and weary,
all whose lives were dreary—
not to the stable only
     Christ came down.

To the humble maiden
     Christ came down;
to the heavy laden
     Christ came down;
hearts chafed sore with sadness
learned to sing with gladness—
not to the stable only
     Christ came down.

To us also, lowly,
     Christ came down—
to our lives unholy
     Christ came down—
to our sorrow bending,
to our pain descending—
not to Bethlehem only
     Christ came down.

LORD, now lettest thou
thy servant depart in PEACE
for mine eyes have seen thy
SALVATION

Luke 2:29-30

Simeon

Once more to the temple, then,
threading the noisy streets
thick with the stench of beasts and men,
festering with deceits—
what is it I came to do,
weary old man, slow of step, dull of eye—
what are you leading me to,
Spirit of the Most High?

Only to feel the chill of age in my bones,
only to see the beggar's angry tears
and the face of the seller of doves, hard and rough as the stones,
and crazy old Anna, bowed with her hundred years—
and these two travellers, bringing their child and their trust
(and two doves clutched in their hands) to present to the Lord.
Well, let me go and look at this new–born burden of dust
and this mother whose heart shall be pierced with a sword.

Yes, look, old man, and exult in this winter morn—
see how simply the Lord masters all sin and decay,
how love invades the dust, to be born and be born and be born.
This is Messiah, this is my promised day,
and I, Simeon, though my hands shake, my eyes fail,
Lord, I have seen thy salvation, and so let my labor cease—
only let me cradle the flesh of God in my frail
            old arms, and then depart in peace.

he took the young CHILD
and his mother by night,
and departed into EGYPT
Matthew 2:14

Joseph in Sinai

I

Huddled against the warmth of a weary beast,
      thankful to be alive, cold and alone
             in a place of stone—
only the hoarse dust in the wind's voice,
the moonlight bare and cold on Sinai's sand;
before dawn we must rise,
      turn our faces from the east,
         and find a refuge under foreign skies.
Yet, the whisper of dust in the wind's moan,
         saying "rejoice, rejoice."
How little of all this I understand.

II

I dreamed we labored through a desert long,
and carried in cupped hands, as in a bowl,
a pulsing heart, as fragile as a song—
and we must neither sleep nor eat nor stay
                          on our appointed way
till we had borne it to its destined goal,
and planted tenderly in sand and stone
                          where from its stain is grown
          a tree that filled the desert sky
          and made the harsh world green with life and grace—
then we lay down in peace, to pray and die.

And I awoke in this forsaken place
          and saw the woman sleeping in my arm,
          the child asleep, secure from harm,
          the moon of Sinai shining on his lovely face.

III

Yes, I remember, in my hurt and shame,
I raged at God, why trial should come to me
                more than to other men—
but the Lord God, wiser than I could be,
burdened and trusted me, and gave
into my human hands this holy life to save.

Farewell to Nazareth, then.
Since I have trusted God as far as Bethlehem,
through Herod's madness and through Sinai's wild,
        I can endure in Egypt, trusting Him.
I learn by trusting where my path must go—
        to spend my strength in shelter of this child.
What he must do for God, as yet I do not know—
        my work is to endure and praise His name.
                For this work I came.

...but we glory in

tribulations also...

Romans 5:3

When We Go Down to Bethlehem...

When we go down to Bethlehem
      in memory or prayer,
our hearts fill grateful to the brim
      that Christ will meet us there—
our words are praise, our song is hymn,
      and all we find is fair.

But in uncertain desert reaches,
      where the heart is chafed with grief,
even the firm of faith beseeches
      strength and courage and relief—
our hope blunts out, our trust runs dry—
      "Where is your comfort now?" we cry.

Lord, let us all our pilgrimage
      walk in the Savior's ways,
till grief and trial, age by age,
      grow testaments of grace—
all flesh a temple of the Lord
      and every breath his praise.

Jesus, thou son of David,
have MERCY on me

Mark 10:47

Prayer for Our Time

Send me thy mercy, Christ—sore is my need.
Cold is my joy, colder than Judah's night,
fevered my hatreds, fierce as Herod's spite,
wasted with hunger no mere flesh can feed,
sick of the darkness, fearful of the light,
in my black sky no star to guide aright—
wayfaring, shelterless, in shame I plead,
find me a stable cleansed of lust and greed.

O gentle Jesus Christ, if once you lowly,
lovely housed in Bethlehem's narrowest rooms,
greater my grief now, more is my life unholy,
O seek and find me here, be born again,
not in a manger, but among the tombs—
Lord, I am legion, and I would be sane.

He hath sent me
to heal the brokenhearted
to preach deliverance to
the captives
and recovering of
sight to the blind
to set at LIBERTY
them that are bruised
to preach the
acceptable year
of the
LORD

Luke 4:18-19

Evangel

O hungry people, feeding as you must
on roots or refuse or mere memory,
who scoop your drink from rainpools laced with dust
and sleep in random shelter fitfully,
just for this Christmas, think of Christ again,
who gave his body for your drink and bread—
        eat, drink, be comforted—
just for today, be filled, lay by your pain.

O restless people, addicts of despair,
spending your selfhood for what cannot please,
who sleep in boredom and rise up in care,
sifting the poor world's wealth for your hearts' ease,
just for this Christmas, think of Christ again,
stilling the riotous waves of Galilee—
        who says, "O weary, come to me"—
just for today, be stilled, lay by your pain.

O Christian people, thoughtless in delight,
clutching your precious gift in secret pride,
debating doctrine while the world bleeds white,
or passing gently on the other side—
just for this Christmas, think of Christ again,
who loved us all when we were spent and lost,
        even at cruel cost—
share with the ruined world your joy, and ease their pain.

I will bring the blind by a
way that they knew not
I will lead them in paths that
they have not known
I will make darkness light
before them   and
                        crooked
                        things
                        straight

Isaiah
42:16

Epiphany

Within the sound of Mary's song,
the harlot huddled in a door,
who had forgotten hope so long
she never would remember more—
the beggar slept in the windy street,
swaddled in rags, against the wall,
and never thought that near his feet
a king slept in a cattle stall.
He sold his pride by bits for drink,
she sold her body for her bread—
and no one gave them any thing.
The seeds of life and joy are dead—
buy as they will, they cannot earn
sufficient misery to think
where in the maze of grief to turn—
what is that grace, who is that king,
whose flesh is broken in their stead.

The miser who by candle–light
picking for meaning in his hoard
turned the vagrants from his sight
had not the wit to know his Lord.
Herod the Great had not the might,
who thought the stars in his control—
he lost his kingdom in the night,
scared by a cradle and a scroll.
And scholars seeking Christ afar,
bringing him gifts revered by men,
would not have found him in a den
without the guidance of a star.

The secret that the angels told
(that he who runs may read it plain)
could not be found by human pain,
could not be got by power or gold,
nor wisdom learned at any cost,
nor any thought men could employ.
But God is wise, though we were lost—
and Jesus Christ, who loved us so,
because we could not reach his joy
bent down to share our woe.

singing and making melody
in your heart to the Lord....

Ephesians 5:19

Music at Christmas

Windy, bleak, and cold,
Christmas comes again this year.
I trudge the busy street,
sludge of the day beneath my feet,
scraps of a shopworn carol in my ear—
  and suddenly I'm four years old
  in a country church, on Daddy's knee—
in a memory clear as a snowfield in the sun,
two voices make two melodies that twine and meld as one—
and heaven and nature sing again for me,
  in my heart a rose blooms red
  out of a stalk I thought was dead.

Oh loving Lord,
I know the day will come
when I can find no word
To make a psalm for you
When cadences go dumb
and metaphors are soiled and few.
  Lord, in that day
  take not your harmonies away.

But when our words go wrong,
send us a phrase of song—
when bard and sage go mute
speak through the argument of the flute—
speak in the eloquence of bells
  where language fails.
Come tune the stammer that we make
even for our lowly Savior's sake,
that in the ashes of the soul
the birth of Jesus Christ may burn like a living coal.

And lo the star... came and stood over where the young child was

Matthew 2:9

Star Carol

The stars look down on human care
untouched, untroubled, unaware,
too far removed to think upon,
cold and chaste as a winter dawn,

so frugal of their precious light
it hardly matters to the night—
clouded by tears, we scarcely see—
little have stars to do with me.

But I know a star that came to stand
by a stable in a sorrowing land,
lending a glow to stumbling feet
where the light of the world and the darkness meet

I know a star that dared the gloom
of a borrowed crib and a felon's tomb—
fire of eternity, refined
to a burning joy in an alien mind.

Ho, every one that thirsteth,
come ye to the waters,
and he that hath no money,
come ye, buy and eat

Isaiah 55:1

Purchase

(Isaiah 55:1 – 2)

I know a treasure hid in a stable
unguarded, unnoticed, yours for the taking,
will buy you a kingdom, will buy you a pardon,
will make you the richest felon on earth.
Starlight and angels will point you the way.

I know a field you can buy worth the money,
rocky, hilly, infested with thorns, but
seeded with diamonds, sown with rubies,
and one great pearl of inestimable price.
Buy it in haste, and gather at leisure—
I know a broker will bargain for you.

>   (Why will you buy the trash the world,
>   why forage on hunger, why gorge on sorrow?
>   I know an inn where you eat without money,
>   buy wine and milk and the bread of life.
>   I know a host will wash your feet—
>   come and feast in an upper room.)

I know a weaver whose loom is the sunlight
will weave you a robe without ever a seam.
His warp is eternity, his woof creation—
he'll spangle you stars on a sable field.

>   (I know a riddle hid in a parable
>   certain as sin, simple as life,
>   will open the vault where wisdom keeps
>   will muddle the mind of many a thinker
>   but children know, and all the forgiven.)

I know a craftsman, a master carpenter,
will build you a house will stand in a storm.
His plumb is straight, his level exacting,
he knows the use of hammer and nails.
He will plane you a stubborn timber,
his crossbeam will bear the weight of the world.

...a man approved of God
among you by miracles and
wonders and signs
                    Acts 2:22

And This Shall Be a Sign...

If Bethlehem could be,
if a star could burn in a cattle stall,
we can be pure again, God loves us after all

angels can carol, if they choose
in any comer of the firmament
Christ can shine in tinsel in a tenement

or ride with reindeer, or in children's laughter
ring peals of parable, or chant a canticle,
ruler of the real and the unreal.
No reasonable mind confines a miracle

...compassed about with
so great a cloud of
witnesses....
Hebrews 12:1

For Those Who Wait

(Psalm 134; Luke 1:19; Hebrews 11)

Watchers, who wait, who stand
all night in the darkened temple,
lift your hands and bless the Lord from Zion,
making the cold stones echo the psalm of the king
stand steadfast: Christ will come.

Prophets, who preach His word
strong–voiced at the city's portals,
shout "Thus saith the Lord" through jeers and stoning—
wilderness–wind–burned, sing of the highway of God
strong–visioned; Christ will come.

Beggars, who brave the chill,
piecemeal in a rusty barrel
fire your zeal with scraps of stolen lumber—
heartened by cheap wine, bold in the flickering light,
hope fiercely; Christ will come.

Shepherds, who shelter lambs
new–born from the cruel winter,
live your praise to God in simple labor—
type of the Lord Christ, wait for the angels' hymn,
watch wondering; Christ will come.

Christian, who chose His way
some time in your tangled sinhood,
drag your cross exulting up Golgotha,
shoulder the bruised world, follow the stain of His steps—
be faithful; Christ will come.

Gabriel, God's good page,
stand ready when he shall beckon,
you who wait forever in His presence—
listen, we plead, fail not when the Lord shall command,
"Go down, let Christ be born."

Said I not unto thee, that
if thou wouldest believe,
thou shouldest see the
glory of God?
John 11:40

Interventions

("Why, who makes much of a miracle?" —Walt Whitman)

A girl may go to a well
and while she is drawing water for the house
she is aware of an angel, sitting there,
saying "Ave, blessed one, the Lord is with thee"

A man may watch by a meager fire
dull from the cold, resigned to grief, and
suddenly, between a drowse and fitful sleep
waken to bright chorales

A man may plot his life with craft and care
dress down his hopes to drab reality
and while he is stacking shekels, one may come
and touch his hand, and murmur "follow me"

A man may trudge an empty street, some casual Christmas,
may turn aside, though callous, to take shelter
where a crude door creaks on a dry hinge in a gritty wind
and find, in a cattle crib, a lovely child.

Except a corn of wheat fall into the ground and die, it abideth alone; but if it die, it bringeth forth much fruit. John 12:24

Dialogue

"... Thou shalt never wash my feet" (John 13:8)

Never, Lord of Life,
may your Holy Fame
welter in our strife,
soil itself in human shame –

never be God's might
swaddled in a human caul
let not Heavenly Light
smolder in a cattle stall.

"Child, you purpose well,
but you do not know
how a seed must burst its shell
if it grow.

If I cannot bear
the Judaean chill,
how endure thorn and spear
on Golgotha's hill?

If I go not down
where the cattle dwell,
how bring back my own
from the pit of hell?

If I do not dare
Herod's bloody sword,
can I come to share
comfort in a cancer ward?

Just where hatreds ramp,
love stands meek and stark—
I must set the lamp
where the house is dark.

Therefore, Earth, make room,
for I shall this day
tear from sorrow's womb
man's eternal joy."

And suddenly... a multitude
of the heavenly host....
Luke 2:9

Aria

This time, no graven stone,
no prophet's shouted word —
no doctrine in syntax alone
however framed, however heard,
can catch the sense, or sum
the rapture of this psalm—
rather, through the midnight calm,
exuberant minstrels come.

Spontaneous the design
of their ethereal mirth —
no need of clef or line,
no more than maps of earth.
Attentive stand the stars, among
horizons of myriad choirs—
such reckless joy requires
not eloquence, but song.

Walk while ye have the light, lest darkness come upon you.

John 12:35

Light

(John 1:4)

dark was the road to Bethlehem
    that crisp Judea night
but Joseph found a way for them
    by soft unearthly light

dark was the crib of Mary's boy
    grievous the labor done
but from her pain there bloomed a joy
    brilliant as the sun

dark the way where the plodding beast
    carried the sage so far
who left the safe and darkening east
    to trust a wandering star

dark was the blood that Herod spilled
    to kill a heavenly king
but faithful luminous grace had willed
    to soothe our suffering

dark, dark, Golgotha's slope
    when God's own flesh was torn
but death burned out in searing hope
    on Resurrection morn

and dark, dark our heart, our mind,
    blind as a clod, a stone,
had Christ not walked as humankind
    and God's redemption shone.

...to seek and to save
that which was lost
Luke 19:10

Beast Fable

I heard the ram at Christmastide
say to the ox who lay beside,
"What guest is this who makes his bed
among the fodder we are fed?"

"The Lord, who took this lowly road
to show us we are loved of God,
that even those in form of beast
are yet invited to his feast.

But he is just a moment lent,
and is on bitter journey bent,
and far beyond our shed must go,
even as far as human woe.

He must descend beneath our stall,
lower than the animal,
below the ravenous wolf and bear,
deep as the hunger of despair."

My Kingdom is not of
This World
John 18:36

Crystal Creche

Domes of the little town of Bethlehem,
the streets, the stable, the transcending star,
adorn my desk—the oxen in their stall,
the Christ-child in his cradle, Joseph, Mary,
shepherds, angels, the whole miracle
made static and translucent as a window,
caught by the craftsman, frozen in their places
in "twenty-four percent full leaded crystal."

Savior, thus my casual generation
has shaped your advent to our greed and revel,
confined the mystery, marketed the beauty–
we mumble prayers or drone our sleepy hymns
or shuffle through our meager charities
or write our poems. Jesus, may your coming
shatter the brittle forms where we entomb
your loveliness, and melt our hearts in praise.

The Son
of
Man
hath not
where

to
lay
his
head

Matthew
8:20

Homeless

"Foxes have holes, the birds of the air have nests,
but the Son of Man nowhere to lay his head"–
only a fodder-trough behind the inn,
only a hurried flight from Herod's rage;
only the dusty by-ways of Judea,
only the silence of Gethsemane garden,
only a lonely watch-tower on Golgotha,
only a rock-hewn tomb in the garden of Joseph–

only the mansions of my father's house.
only the praise of Michelangelo,
only the hush of a million congregations,
only the peace and prayer of a godly household,
only the love of publicans and lepers,
only the hopes of children who live in holes,
only our swept and ordered lives, Lord Jesus.

As one whom his mother comforteth, so will I comfort you

Isaiah 66:13

New York Christmas, 2001

Fierce lights filter through the smoke, and snow
sifting through concrete dust, through human ash,
settles on steel skeletons still groping
an open void that was a stairwell, sifting
through memories, thousands of hovering ghosts,
swirling through smoke touching smoldering rubble,
touching somber faces, touching careful groping hands
that sift the ash, that sort the shards and dust
searching, searching relics, searching solace,
searching peace on earth.
                              Soon may the snow
swaddle all, in a white innocence,
the soft and sifting lovely silent snowfall
 soothing the angry tangled ruined world.

Blessed are the Poor in Spirit
for theirs is the Kingdom of
Heaven
Matthew 5:3

Pastoral

Make a wee fire, lad,
we've a bitter night.
Hands and heart are numb—
kindle us warmth and light.

Weary hours to watch
until the morning sun—
our ewe must drop her lamb
before our labor's done.

Birth and labor and death,
a shepherd's daily bread—
his sign, a rod and staff—
no place to lay his head.

When the Messiah comes,
they say, he'll set us free—
but laddie, he'll not come
to such as you and me.

Temple or palace, lad,
clean linen for his rest—
the praise of priest and king,
the banquets of the blest.

And lad, all joy to him,
no blessing is too much.
All labor and grief be ours,
if we can spare him such.

Amen, let it be so—
his power and praise be great!
Kindle a fire, my boy,
we'll watch the stars, and wait.

A well of water
springing up into
Everlasting Life
John 4:14

The Hanging of the Green

Bare limbs moan in a gusty wind,
sun and cloud grow blue with cold,
frozen brook and black rocks blend,
fern and flower are withered to mould–
all living things to ice and stone decline
except this stubborn green of mistletoe and pine.

So wintry minds, by custom grown
impervious to mystery,
contented with the banal known,
smother the struggle to break free–
snuggled down in their familiar bark,
secured from sharp epiphany by insulating dark.

So grief-arrested feelings hide
their pulse of life in ice-bound springs
to callous over shame and pride
until the grace of Jesus brings
a surge of promise, as fresh waters risen
from deep artesian sources thaw and burst their prison.

Bring the green branches to our halls.
Their living thread assures rebirth
in oak and elm and frozen falls–
green hope sustains the dormant earth.
Just so, the startling joy of Christmas morn
sings to the catatonic heart, Rejoice, the Lord is born.

He that giveth,
let him do it with simplicity
Romans 12:8

Gifts of the Magi

A gift is not gift
        that bribes reward or pardon
        or brags its wealth, or states its condescension;

for gold is only gold
        until alloyed with worship
        burnished with love and joy in others' gladness

and costly frankincense
        perfumes the giver only
        unless we break this alabaster body.

Myrrh only lengthens grief
        unless a stubborn trusting
        can bury sorrow as the seed of dawning.

Wisely the kings of old
        abandoned self, to honor
        our Savior's birth, and labor, and his dying.

Second Coming

What if he came again,
not in what men call glory, but in shame,
      just as before he came–
would we know him, then?

Let's say he showed up sleeping in the street,
scrounging for whatever's thrown away,
scraping a lunch the wasteful didn't eat,
saving a biscuit for another day–

or say he's some kid in the neighborhood
whose dad's in prison for about ten years,
and people hint his mother's not too good
(he keeps alone so no one sees his tears)

or he'd be preaching in the park, some wild
new oracle from Jonah, at noonday–
harmless, I guess—innocent as a child,
but clearly crazy—should be put away–

or standing on a bridge at dark, and staring
fixedly at the river far below him
as if unsure if heaven or earth was caring–
if someone said "That's Jesus!"–would we know him?

But thou,
Bethlehem,
though thou
be little ... yet
out of thee shall he come
to be Ruler in Israel
Micah 5:2

Dialogue in Herod's Palace

"My good friend Balthazar,
something is evil in the courts of Judah.
The palace guards are sullen,
servants and beggars mutter imprecations.
The very dogs cringe and run away.
This king who speaks of worship is a liar.
His priests and counselors are afraid of him.
His eyes are cold, his garments reek of blood.
Surely this is a kingdom built on death.

So have we trudged the desert and the wadis
to find our newborn king in such a land?"

"Not here, my friend–
rather in some humble cleanly place.
One more brief pilgrimage, if God gives strength,
before we die, to find and worship him,
and then at length our labor finds an end.
The star that led us promised peace and grace.
Come, let us go to Bethlehem."

Everyone
who thirsts,

come
to
the
Waters

Isaiah 55:1

Coming to Bethlehem

For some, through years of search and censure,
enticed by facile visions in our youth,
surrendering in sorrow many a winsome truth
       sweet to the taste, bitter to the heart,
       watching them one by one default and part,
we plod with patient hope the logic of antiquities,
       until at last, among their mysteries,
a flash of brilliance where no steady mind should venture–
          startled from circumspection,
          dare trust beyond confusion
          call to a reckless mission.

For some, in everyday sufficiency,
unsure what other choice we must forgo,
compelled by Caesar where we would not go–
       jostling other pilgrims for a bed,
       finding at last a drafty shed,
enduring stench of other beasts, enduring dark and cold,
       struggling, against our rebel flesh, to hold
          by trust alone his promise in a vague epiphany–
          there finding, to our ardor,
          glory unashamed to harbor
          as fruit of body's labor.

Some, with soiled and calloused hands, with soil
in calloused souls, the desperate of the race,
no claim or expectation of God's grace,
       slaves to a starveling livelihood
       whether of spirit or of food,
resigned to darkness, shivering want, daily crust,
       the rancid joys allowed mere human dust,
humbled to gratitude for thankless toil–
          invaded suddenly by holy clamor,
          invited to a stable yonder,
          feast on extravagant splendor.

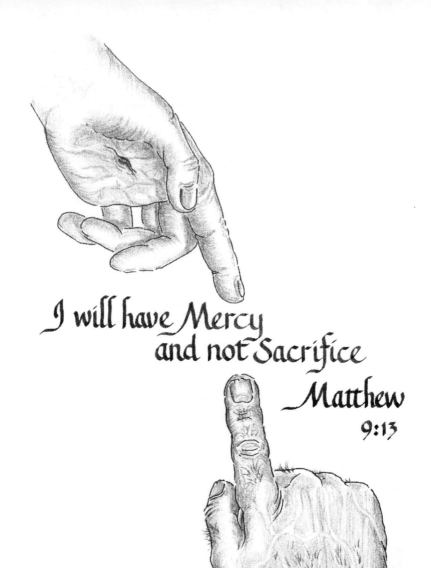

I will have Mercy
and not Sacrifice

Matthew
9:13

Flesh

Year upon bloody year,
man offers goat or lamb
in holy rite of fear,
not knowing who I am.

As if to prove to me
how cruel flesh can be.

Slave to his shame and lust,
his god can be no less.

How then to cleanse and bless?
How can I renew
mutual love and trust
we once in Eden's evening knew?

I must come down and live as dust.
No other way for them to see
how holy flesh can be.

Afterword

And so, after 36 years, I will lay down this enterprise of discovery and praise. I will not lay down the blessing, but try to turn it to other expressions.

What I have learned is that the incarnation of God in Jesus the Christ is the statement of all Scripture, the source of peace and strength in human experience, the essence of God's purpose toward his creation, especially toward his human children.

This is what I take from the story of Jesus' coming. However we have distorted it in our faulty observance, faniciful mythology, self-interested interpretation, God will forgive the flaws, if we persevere in our effort to understand.

At least, so it has proved for me. I hope that it may also be a blessing for you.

Bill Mitchell